W9-ARF-116

Community Workers

A Carpenter's Job

Erika de Nijs

Cavendish
Square

New York

Published in 2016 by Cavendish Square Publishing, LLC
243 5th Avenue, Suite 136, New York, NY 10016

Copyright © 2016 by Cavendish Square Publishing, LLC

First Edition

Website: cavendishsq.com

This publication represents the opinions and views of the author based on his or her personal experience, knowledge, and research. The information in this book serves as a general guide only. The author and publisher have used their best efforts in preparing this book and disclaim liability rising directly or indirectly from the use and application of this book.

CPSIA Compliance Information: Batch #WS15CSQ

All websites were available and accurate when this book was sent to press.

Library of Congress Cataloging-in-Publication Data

de Nijs, Erika.
A carpenter's job / Erika de Nijs.
pages cm. — (Community workers)
Includes bibliographical references and index.
ISBN 978-1-50260-428-6 (hardcover) ISBN 978-1-50260-427-9 (paperback) ISBN 978-1-50260-429-3 (ebook)
1. Wooden-frame buildings—Vocational guidance—Juvenile literature. 2. Building, Wooden—Vocational guidance—Juvenile literature.
3. Carpenters—Juvenile literature. I. Title.

TH1101.N45 2016
694.023—dc23

2014050269

Editorial Director: David McNamara
Editor: Fletcher Doyle
Copy Editor: Cynthia Roby
Art Director: Jeffrey Talbot
Designer: Alan Sliwinski
Senior Production Manager: Jennifer Ryder-Talbot
Photo Research by J8 Media
Production Editor: Renni Johnson

Photos by: Kzenon/Shutterstock.com, cover; Tyler Olson/Shutterstock.com, 5; Isantilli/Shutterstock.com, 7; bikeriderlondon/Shutterstock.com, 9; Tyler Olson/Shutterstock.com, 11; Dmitry Kalinovsky/Shutterstock.com, 13; michaeljung/Shutterstock.com, 15; Huntstock/Getty Images, 17; Brightrock/iStockphoto.com, 19; Andresr/Shutterstock.com, 21.

Printed in the United States of America

Contents

I am a carpenter.

I build things with wood.

4

5

I use tools.

I measure, cut, drill, and sand wood.

I wear **goggles** to protect my eyes.

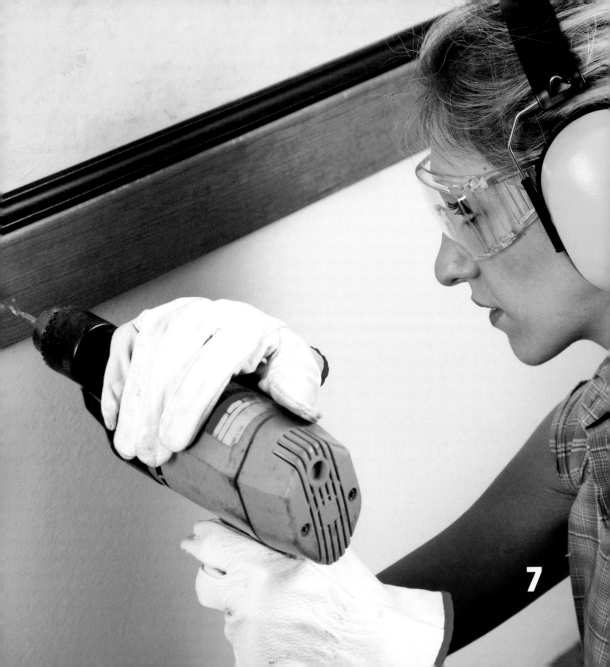

7

I can build a house.

The house will have lots
of windows.

A family will love living in it.

9

I make sure that things are **level**.

This will keep you safe.

10

11

Roofs wear out and leak.

I can replace your roof to keep you dry.

I **hammer** in nails quickly.

12

13

I put together **cabinets** and bookshelves.

14

15

Sometimes I work high above the ground.

I carry my tools in a belt.

I wear a **hard hat**.

17

Some carpenters make furniture and cabinets.

18

19

Your house is done.

You can move in now!

20

New Words

cabinet (CAB-eh-neht) Furniture with shelves or drawers used to keep things in.

goggles (GAHG-gulz) Glasses that fit tightly and are made to protect your eyes.

hard hat (HARD HAT) A sturdy hat worn by workers for safety.

hammer (HAM-murr) To hit something with a hammer. This is a tool with a heavy head and a handle.

level (LEH-vul) Something that is flat and even.

Index

About the Author

Erika de Nijs played college hockey before becoming a teacher and a writer. Her parents are from the Netherlands but she grew up in Upstate New York.

About BOOK WORMS

Bookworms help independent readers gain reading confidence through high-frequency words, simple sentences, and strong picture/text support. Each book explores a concept that helps children relate what they read to the world in which they live.